# Body Voices

Kevin Reid

# Body Voices

Poems © 2013 by Kevin Reid

Cover art by Steven B. Smith
http://agentofchaos.com

## Crisis Chronicles #39

Published 10 February 2013
ISBN: 978-0-9857897-8-7

Crisis Chronicles Press
John Burroughs, editor
3344 W. 105th Street #4
Cleveland, Ohio 44111
United States of America

http://press.crisischronicles.com &
facebook.com/crisischroniclespress

For Manna

# Preface

Within this supplement of words you will find:

An old boar
Kali's hands
A free sinner
Heart attacks
Speaking hair
An open stage
A talking brain
Stunned lungs
A hungry child
A catholic boy
Footloose feet
Strained veins
A curious finger
Cannibal bandits
A Tantric Buddhist
A bionic pensioner
The womb of Zeus
Nipples as an extra
Naked exhibitionists
A bald headed egoist
A discontinued sweet
Shape shifting strangers
And an impressive belly button.

# Eyes

Of similar size since
the womb pushed me out to see,

my mother's brown irises,
the blue of my father's,

their young parent smiles
and early sixties hairstyles.

...visual dementia...

At birth the eyes are canonized
then the mind leads them astray.

My eyes I realise
are much older than me.

I remain ignorant to their wisdom.

## Nose

*It fits in*

    *and*

        *sticks out.*

            It points
to the world.

On my face like a curious finger
it touches the air.

Upon the open stage above my top lip
nature's perfumed players perform
a scented dance

    In

    and

    out...

Hyacinth harmonies play silently.

# Ears

*Once upon a time ... easy chairs*
for parental voices.

In rebellious adolescence,
hanging eager by the wayside,
they stood out like naked exhibitionists
waiting for the next banging response.

Perpetual voices of numerous narrators:

the babble of baby-talk,
the nameless noise of childhood,
the screeching cries of my newborn,
the giggling cruel capers of a lover's infidelity

all strained through dunes of skin and bone.

In the *change of life*
these ever growing flower heads of flesh
pollinate my head with the white noise of tinnitus

and I shrink.

# Mouth

In the north of the body there's a state called the head
where the entire southern coastline is a magical forest;
when chopped back in summer it grows back in winter.

Before the forest was planted
friends and families would gather
round this open stage.

In summer a growing cast
of full on and frontal young artistes
would expose themselves in performance:

*Dancing on Gum,*
*Grinding with Speed,*
*A Visit to the Dentist.*        (only when in need)

In winter, rattled together, the vocal
point of conversation was splitting
ideas of old productions and new:

*Please Release Me, Let Me Go,* possibly a plaque winner,
*When Things Were Rotten,* served with a complimentary dinner,
*Shake, Rattle 'n' Roll,* wearing nothing on the whole,
*Between the Laughter,* could win them a BAFTA,

When I arrived the stage was hidden
by curtains faded and creased,
I opened them gently.

With bones showing,
their costumes worn and stained,
and no longer dazzling the crowd
with their full frontal performance,
the senescent cast hangs
rigid from the receding heavens
and lie rotting in the stalls.                                    →

11

*On the whole*
my mouth makes a tasteful effort,
inviting productions of pleasure:
food, smoke, booze and a kiss.

However, my tongue can be a prick,
                    "Fuckin' this and fuckin' that ..."


## Brain

I'm a complex institute of numerous faculties,
where learning awakes with a yawn,
energy is monopolised by maintenance
and thinking hard is barely discernible.

I'm a hardback tome bound in bone,
spine lined and stitched with nerves.
Void of font my volumes in cerebrum read a
testament of human speech and language.

I'm an expansive mansion of cortex corridors
decked with memories and hopes hereafter,
with a manual motor sitting in the spinal drive:
the volunteers of human movement.

I'm psychedelic fruit cradled in a cranium,
a blood ripe pink avocado to the touch.
I'm a giant walnut wrinkled to the eye,
lucid in the absence of hallucinogens.

I'm treasured by several states, a crown jewel,
a gleam in the eye of the commander-in-chief,
a spark in the cavity of his war machine,
a hidden gem in the hands of the pacifist.

I'm a small mute reptile, ancient survivor.
I'm a fist in a fight dominant with rage.
I'm the wings for flight, engine of control.
I'm the instinctive master of mating.

I'm a masked genius with a desire
to learn the truth of myself, who
knows all, doesn't feel,
yet can be fooled.

## Heart

It was our anniversary. I felt alive and well
suffering only a slight coronary a year ago.

I caught the look of panic in her loving face
as I collapsed with chronic chest pains.

I recall the fast arrival of green paramedics
and the pound of my pulse as it returned.

Moments later another attack and another
and another and another five times again.

Still, my pulse came back with saving shocks
and my blood ran with an anti-clot injection.

Three further arrests then flown to hospital,
*never known the need for twelve shocks.*

*Incredible… a non-smoker,*
a stent put in place and kept in for six days.

Back home and doing well they said
It took *forty* minutes to save his life.

# Nipples

These parched pits; useless
reminders of *man's* misfortune.

Dried up wells
on this ageing wasteland;
an early design with no future in mind.

In *man's* life there's a landscape
where nature offers fertilit(y)
and gives nipples as an e(x)tra.

Pocket studs on this male garment;
barely high fashion. Remnants
of the female I was in the beginning.

In *utero* there was an e(x)clusive junction
where nature didn't ask wh(y) and
gave *man* the change.

Two old pennies; worthless
souvenirs from the womb.

Once I met a woman
who offered me a pleasing price
                    just to pinch them.

# Lungs

**I**

Chest pains
— cancer!

Surgeons opened me
— stunned!

In dampness
and darkness

firm, healthy
bright green needles:

a five centimetres spruce
with no roots.


**II**

War
left you breathless.

A transplant
to save your life.

A year later
in your fifty a day
*new lungs* — a tumour.

# Hands

**I**

They touch me up with mythology.

Kali, a night time dancer,
allures and enchants with
her polymeliac dance, wanks
me with her lower hands and
whispers in my ear,
              "You shouldn't cum here".


**II**

They talk to me of synaesthesia.

The thumb and the baby finger:
ears swollen with grasp.

The ring and index finger:
eyes worn with a pointed stare.

The middle finger:
a nose sticking out from all the rest.

The palm:
a mouth open to receive and open to give.

## Stomach

Schools closed. The strikes.
It makes no difference,
school is almost childless
these days. They don't bother to come.

My grandparents are tired,
aunties and uncles too.
Drought's tough, farms fail
these days. No work and little to eat.

We're up early to hunt. Wild
fruit to share and mealie meal
from the miller. Today I scraped 2 kilos.

Life is hard in Zimbabwe,
I do most of the running.
I tried to thieve some biscuits
today. I'm not sorry I'm hungry.

## Navel

The belly button
impresses, twists a recall
not tied with the world.

# Penis

**penis** *n. the male organ of copulation ...also used for urine excretion...*

I come to the Pubis region,
it's dark. The point?
To make peace with my penis.

Infamous this bald headed egoist
in and out the city of Genitalia
shooting up in any alleyway he can find.

Above all a hard man in the morning

At dawn          I move quietly towards him.

Relaxed and sunken
he sleeps on his wrinkled bean bag.

Suddenly with thrust he stands erect
and sets the ball(s) rolling.

Launching into his space travel thrills
(*One of man's greatest ...?*)
in the cockpit of a supersonic jet thrusting
upwards and heading all the way for Venus.

Banging on about his religious experience
(*One of man's greatest ...?*)
as an organist in a church warmed up
and pumping he played *Lay Lady Lay*.

Coming over with his youthful shenanigans
humping on a sink and rushing to a climax
he lost his virginity in a public toilet then

wrote upon the wall,

*When my penis first landed on Venus*                    →

*I felt like a fuckin' genius*
*I stood tall and inflated*
*wholly elated,*
*but don't let that come between us.*

Beating on and on the point came
when my head was throbbing
and ready to explode!

The upshot?
My penis: a wanker,
a sex junkie who often talks piss.

# Thighs

Flummoxed by the femur
I lose impetus
utter function strikes me silent.

Still I walk in their company.

I meet Genesis and Exodus and I am told
when a hand is placed under the thigh and
the mission held true sterility may not be born;
proof in the womb of Zeus.

Still I walk in their company.

I meet a child fast pedalling a bicycle,
his right thigh bitten by a dog named *Boot*
with a weak master and no collar or chain.

Still I walk in their company.

I meet a Tantric Buddhist evoking spirit.
Accompanied by the damaru he plays
the kangling with his left hand to
drive away evil and cut off the ego.

Still with support of their company
I am urged to talk the walk of
these masters in momentum.

# Buttocks

*...floating symbols...never representing themselves...*

Joined at the hip,
muscular yet humble, these shape shifting strangers
take me to the hindquarters show me to my seat
then breach my brain with joy and pain.

Pygopagus dazzles its prey with its twin moons
and lashes their butts with two wicked whips
as it hits its desired destination for painful lessons.

The anger in my father's eyes
the firm hiding of his leather belt
for stealing apples and shitting myself.

The Devil bites a pact with a witch and
leaves his mark: the twisted horns of a ram.
This fiendish Callipygian:
the wet dream of a young pygophilist.

The excitement of my first grope
behind the bush by the burn
her bare butt and her birthmark.

Joined at the hip,
muscular yet humble, these shape shifting strangers
take me to the hindquarters show me to my seat
and expose me to the art and arse of fashion.

19th Century:
the outstanding celebration of the bustle revealed
on a *Sunday Afternoon on the Island of La Grande Jatte*.

21st Century:
the coin slot of the fashion conscious hooker
and the shame of her vertical smile in return.

Fuck that.

As I leave by the back passage I catch wind of an ancient tale
about a dominatrix who spanked her clients scarlet before
some arse slapped their raw rump on the scales of Libra
and sold it to the masses as astrology.

Enough of that crap.

I shit by the rear entrance,
my horizontal smile as I recall these signifiers of seat,
this mechanism of motion that gives way to excretion
and revealed the goddess to Virgil.

# Knees

Innocent
catholic boy
his Sunday best
naively knelt in pews
gave thanks for being blessed

modest
catholic boy
his bended knees
bore bruises for religion
knuckled down at the altar in prayer

humble
catholic boy
his stained soul
honoured the free sinner
rejected the purity in priesthood

vulnerable
catholic boy
his sinister stance
broken by belief
kneecapped by christ's criminals

submissive
catholic boy
his naked knees
flirted with a thirsty virgin
encountered erotic empathy

curious
catholic boy
his sexual query
bent the rules for pleasure
worshipped the second coming

disillusioned
catholic boy
prostrates no more
leaves fate to sit
*on the knees of the gods*


## Heels

Where I *take to* and run with hard fear.
When I am just a short palindrome
synonymous with provision.
When money is a callous parental kiss
and precious time a discontinued sweet.

Where I *dig in* and burn with raw anger.
When my sensitive soul is under pressure
from the jack boot of inflamed bureaucracy.
When writing is reduced to report
and precious time a red rag.

Where I *look back* rubbed with sore regret.
When my blushing conscience comes bounding
through a walk in the hills.
When words are litter in the woods
and precious time is just behind.

Where I'm at: worn down and weak.
When the domestic is a marathon
I'm tired of racing.
When home is furnished with bruises
and precious time unkempt.

# Toes

this old boar goes to work
this old boar stays in bed
this old boar has a virtual life
this old boar has none
and this old boar is pitiful

despite being in front
usually first to arrive
they're often not seen
under socked stealth
and cobbled shields

lengthy shifts undercover
this small wiggling workforce
press on with the great
unwashed complement
not quite a fine French

# Feet

step in
at first
useless
and born

        step forth
        with the
        learning
        to walk

step back
with the
instinct
intact

        step down
        with a
        toddler's
        temper

step up
with a
torment
tickle

        step off
        with the
        nettles'
        defence

step on
with the
clinging
dogshit

        step to
        with the
        bully's
        pursuit

→

27

step from
with the
chafing
school shoes

        step up
        with a
        drug dubbed
        dance

step down
with its
stomping
hard cramps

        step here
        with sole
        and bones
        defined

step there
the font
of my
footprints

        step out
        at last
        footloose
        with death

# Skin

**I**

*Perfect day skin begins here!*

*Roll-on cleanse glow*
*prep prime and refine*

*Wake up to the face*
*body and breast revolution*

*Resurface from make-up*
*clinically zapped and scrubbed*

*Age control lifted firmer*
*first line signs absorbed*

*Soft focused full and smooth*
*scars and marks understood*

*"Read my re-plump lips"*
          says Auntie Wrinkle with cosmetic confidence.

**II**

Tales of assassins:
cannibal bandits
ate skin and sold fat.

Scores butchered,
thorax and thighs.

Torsos hang from hooks
fat tubs below
candle warmed flesh.

Amber liquid:
the anti-wrinkle ringleader.

## Bones

Joints crumble
arteries fur
teeth fall.

Hip and knee
surgical implants
scaffold my body.

Stripped of foreign DNA
by blood and transplant,
partners in artificial health.

People:
tangible products,
a series of joints and valve innovations.

"With clinical colonization I could last a lifetime"
says the bionic pensioner.

# Veins

Blood soaked lattice of the neonatal
supporting life through warp and weft.

Swollen blue, crimson flat, silent grey,
strained by an inhaled toxic chain.

Tired, tread and perished, we persist,
puncture repaired with social policies.

We will be the marble in mortals,
the black lace of the decaying corpse.

# Hair

*By the time your hair emerges from under the skin it is dead.*

In death
black
brown
red
and fair.

In death
coarse
grey
thin
and white.

In death we part.

# Appendix

It's often said I've lost my traditional purpose
through the passage of literary evolution,
the theory of my original role in digesting
leaves replaced by the new world idea
of an immune function rich in infection
fighting and maintaining vital flora.

Digested, this supplement of words
and white leaves, full in expression
and verbal flora, offers the bookworm
beneficial bacteria for thought, and
is intended to harbour and protect
creative infection within the reader.

# Acknowledgments

"Thighs" and "Buttocks" published in an earlier form by *Eviscerator Heaven*.

"Eyes" published in an earlier form by *The Plebian Rag*.

Many thanks to John Burroughs, Rich Follett and Gillian Prew.

# Crisis Chronicles Press Titles